AF289529

Maher Asaad Baker

Welcome Mind Challenges

ISBN Softcover: 978-3-384-22856-7

ISBN Hardback: 978-3-384-22857-4

ISBN E-Book: 978-3-384-22858-1

ISBN Large print: 978-3-384-22859-8

Contents

Understanding the Challenges of the Mind 1

Decision Paralysis and Effective Decision-Making Strategies 39

Procrastination and Boosting Productivity 76

Information Overload and Enhancing Focus 101

Emotional Roadblocks and Building Emotional Resilience 118

Confirmation Bias and Expanding Perspectives............................ 145

Multitasking and Cultivating Single-Tasking Skills 169

Overcoming Mind Challenges for Success..................................... 195

Disclaimer 209

About the Author................................**Error! Bookmark not defined.**

Understanding the Challenges of the Mind

In the vast and unpredictable landscape of life, we often encounter obstacles that test our mettle. A strong and resilient mind is the compass that guides us through these trials, enabling us to make sound decisions and persevere in the face of adversity.

Mental fortitude, the unwavering strength of one's mind, is the foundation upon which we build our capacity to overcome life's hurdles. It is the steadfast resolve that propels us forward when we are beset by doubt, fear, or despair.

Cultivating mental fortitude involves embracing challenges, pushing beyond our comfort zones, and nurturing a growth mindset. It requires us to face our fears and insecurities head-on, acknowledging them without allowing them to dictate our actions. By fostering mental fortitude, we equip ourselves with the tools necessary to navigate life's complexities and uncertainties with grace and determination.

Resilience, the ability to adapt and recover from adversity, is the counterpart to mental fortitude. While mental fortitude provides the strength to endure, resilience enables us to bounce back from setbacks and maintain our equilibrium in the face of change.

Cultivating resilience involves developing coping mechanisms, fostering adaptability, and nurturing a positive outlook. It requires us to recognize that setbacks are an inevitable part of life and to view them as opportunities for growth and learning. By embracing resilience, we can navigate life's challenges with agility and poise, emerging from each trial more capable and confident than before.

Mental fortitude and resilience are interconnected, each reinforcing and enhancing the other. A strong and resilient mind is one that can withstand the pressures of life's challenges while maintaining the flexibility to adapt and grow. This delicate balance is essential for navigating the complexities of decision-making and daily life.

In the crucible of adversity, mental fortitude and resilience are forged and tempered. Each challenge we face serves to strengthen our resolve and hone our ability to adapt. By cultivating mental fortitude and resilience, we arm ourselves with the fortitude to fight for our dreams, our values, and our place in the world.

A strong and resilient mind is crucial in the realm of decision-making. The ability to weigh options, consider consequences, and make informed choices is essential for navigating life's challenges. Mental fortitude enables us to remain steadfast in our convictions, while resilience allows us to adapt our plans and strategies as circumstances change.

In the face of uncertainty, a resilient mind can discern the subtle nuances of each situation, identifying opportunities and potential pitfalls. This keen insight allows us to make decisions that are both bold and prudent, balancing risk and reward in pursuit of our goals.

Persistence, the unwavering commitment to a course of action, is a hallmark of a strong and resilient mind.

Cultivating persistence requires patience, discipline, and an unwavering belief in our abilities. It demands that we confront our limitations, learn from our mistakes, and remain steadfast in our pursuit of excellence. By embracing persistence, we demonstrate our commitment to overcoming life's challenges and achieving our goals.

Self-reflection is an essential component of mental fortitude and resilience. It is through introspection that we gain insight into our thoughts, emotions, and behaviors, allowing us to identify patterns, recognize strengths, and address weaknesses.

Self-reflection enables us to strive for continuous improvement, fostering personal growth and development. By cultivating a practice of self-reflection, we nurture our mental fortitude and resilience, equipping ourselves with the tools necessary to navigate life's challenges with confidence and grace.

Mind challenges are the cognitive obstacles that arise from the complex interplay of thoughts, emotions, and beliefs that shape our perception of reality. They can manifest in various forms, such as indecision, procrastination, or the inability to adapt to change. These challenges are often the result of deeply ingrained patterns of thinking and behavior that have developed over time, making them difficult to identify and address.

Decision-making is a critical aspect of our lives, shaping our choices and determining the trajectory of our personal and professional journeys. Mind challenges can significantly impair our ability to make informed and effective decisions, leading to indecision, impulsiveness, or an inability to weigh the consequences of our actions.

One such challenge is the phenomenon of analysis paralysis, wherein an individual becomes overwhelmed by the sheer volume of information and potential outcomes, resulting in an inability to make a decision. This can lead to missed opportunities, stagnation, and a sense of frustration and disempowerment.

Another common challenge is the presence of cognitive biases, which can distort our perception of reality and influence our decision-making processes. Confirmation bias, for example, is the tendency to seek out information that supports our preexisting beliefs while disregarding contradictory evidence. This can lead to flawed decisions based on incomplete or inaccurate information.

Mind challenges can also have a profound impact on our daily routines, affecting our productivity, relationships, and overall well-being. Procrastination, for instance, is a common challenge that can lead to wasted time, increased stress, and a sense of accomplishment.

Multitasking is another challenge that can significantly impair our ability to focus and complete tasks efficiently. While it may seem like an effective way to manage multiple responsibilities, research has shown that multitasking can actually decrease productivity and increase the likelihood of errors.

Emotional intelligence, the ability to recognize, understand, and manage our emotions, plays a crucial role in navigating mind challenges. By cultivating emotional intelligence, we can develop greater self-awareness, empathy, and resilience, enabling us to better understand and address the underlying causes of our cognitive obstacles.

Overcoming mind challenges requires a combination of self-awareness, introspection, and proactive strategies. By developing a deeper understanding of our thought patterns, emotions, and behaviors, we can identify the root causes of our challenges and implement targeted solutions.

Cultivate Mindfulness: Mindfulness is the practice of being present and fully engaged in the current moment, without judgment or distraction. By cultivating mindfulness, we can develop greater self-awareness, enabling us to recognize and address mind challenges as they arise.

Practice Self-Compassion: Self-compassion involves treating ourselves with kindness, understanding, and empathy in the face of adversity. By practicing self-compassion, we can develop greater resilience and the capacity to learn from our experiences, rather than being consumed by self-criticism and doubt.

Set Clear Goals and Priorities: Establishing clear goals and priorities can help us maintain focus and direction in the face of mind challenges. By breaking down our objectives into smaller, manageable tasks, we can create a sense of progress and accomplishment, reducing the likelihood of becoming overwhelmed or disheartened.

Embrace Change and Uncertainty: The ability to adapt to change and uncertainty is a key component of overcoming mind challenges. By cultivating a growth mindset and embracing the unknown, we can develop the flexibility and resilience necessary to navigate the complexities of decision-making and daily life.

Seek Support and Collaboration: Connecting with others can provide valuable insights, perspectives, and encouragement in the face of mind challenges. By seeking support and collaboration, we can foster a sense of community and shared understanding, empowering us to overcome our cognitive obstacles together.

Resilience, the capacity to withstand and recover from adversity, is a vital component of human flourishing. Overcoming mind challenges can forge and strengthen our resilience, enabling us to navigate the complexities of life with greater ease and fortitude.

Confronting and overcoming mind challenges can lead to a deeper understanding of our thoughts, emotions, and behaviors. This heightened self-awareness enables us to recognize patterns, identify strengths, and address weaknesses, fostering personal growth and development. By cultivating a practice of introspection and self-reflection, we can better understand the intricacies of our minds and develop strategies to navigate the challenges that arise.

Emotional intelligence, the ability to recognize, understand, and manage our emotions, is an essential skill in navigating the complexities of human interaction and decision-making. Overcoming mind challenges can enhance our emotional intelligence, allowing us to develop greater empathy, compassion, and self-regulation. By cultivating emotional intelligence, we can foster more meaningful connections with others and make more informed, empathetic decisions.

Adaptability, the ability to adjust and thrive in the face of change, is a key component of success in an ever-evolving world. Overcoming mind challenges can enhance our adaptability, enabling us to approach new situations with flexibility, creativity, and resilience. By embracing change and uncertainty, we can develop the capacity to navigate the complexities of life with agility and poise.

A growth mindset, the belief that our abilities and intelligence can be developed through dedication and hard work, is a powerful catalyst for personal growth and achievement. Overcoming mind challenges can foster a growth mindset, empowering us to view obstacles as opportunities for learning and development. By cultivating a growth mindset, we can unlock our potential, transcending the limitations imposed by fixed beliefs and self-imposed barriers.

Effective decision-making is a critical skill in navigating the complexities of life. Overcoming mind challenges can enhance our decision-making abilities, enabling us to weigh options, consider consequences, and make informed choices with confidence and clarity. By honing our decision-making skills, we can better navigate the intricacies of our personal and professional lives, making choices that align with our values and aspirations.

Overcoming mind challenges can lead to a profound sense of inner peace, as we learn to navigate the tumultuous waters of our thoughts and emotions with greater equanimity. By cultivating a sense of calm and tranquility amidst the chaos, we can develop a deeper connection with ourselves and the world around us, fostering a sense of harmony and well-being.

Confronting and overcoming mind challenges can unleash our creative potential, as we learn to approach problems from new perspectives and devise innovative solutions. By nurturing our creativity, we can unlock our imagination, fostering a sense of wonder and curiosity that enriches our lives and the lives of those around us.

Overcoming mind challenges can provide a sense of purpose and meaning, as we learn to align our actions with our values and aspirations. By pursuing a life of intention and authenticity, we can create a sense of fulfillment and satisfaction, knowing that we are living in accordance with our deepest desires and convictions.

Mind challenges can be temporary or enduring, subtle or overt, and can significantly impact our ability to process information, make decisions, and engage in daily routines. Mind challenges are often the result of deeply ingrained patterns of thinking and behavior that have developed over time, making them difficult to identify and address.

Mind challenges can be categorized into various forms, each with its unique characteristics and implications. The following taxonomy provides an overview of the diverse landscape of cognitive challenges that we may encounter in our lives.

Indecision is a common mind challenge that arises from an inability to make a clear choice among available options. This can lead to analysis paralysis, wherein an individual becomes overwhelmed by the sheer volume of information and potential outcomes, resulting in an inability to make a decision. Indecision can stem from fear of making the wrong choice, lack of self-confidence, or an inability to weigh the consequences of different options effectively.

Procrastination is the act of delaying or postponing tasks, often leading to wasted time, increased stress, and a sense of unfulfillment. This mind challenge can be driven by various factors, such as fear of failure, lack of motivation, or an inability to prioritize tasks effectively. Procrastination can have significant consequences on our productivity, relationships, and overall well-being.

Cognitive biases are systematic errors in thinking that can distort our perception of reality and influence our decision-making processes. These biases can arise from various sources, such as social, cultural, or personal factors, and can lead to flawed judgments and decisions. Examples of cognitive biases include confirmation bias, the tendency to seek out information that supports our preexisting beliefs while disregarding contradictory evidence, and the anchoring effect, the reliance on initial information when making subsequent judgments.

Emotional roadblocks are mind challenges that arise from intense or unresolved emotions, such as fear, anger, or sadness. These emotions can hinder our ability to process information, make decisions, and engage in daily activities. Emotional roadblocks can be the result of past experiences, unresolved conflicts, or underlying mental health issues.

Multitasking is the attempt to perform multiple tasks simultaneously, often leading to decreased productivity and increased errors. While it may seem like an effective way to manage multiple responsibilities, research has shown that multitasking can actually impair our ability to focus and complete tasks efficiently. This mind challenge can arise from an inability to prioritize tasks, a desire to accomplish more in less time, or a lack of self-discipline.

Perfectionism is the relentless pursuit of flawlessness, often leading to self-criticism, procrastination, and burnout. This mind challenge can stem from high personal standards, a fear of failure, or a desire to gain approval from others. Perfectionism can have significant consequences on our mental health, relationships, and overall quality of life.

The fear of change is a mind challenge that arises from an aversion to uncertainty and the unknown. This fear can manifest as resistance to new experiences, reluctance to embrace new ideas, or an unwillingness to adapt to changing circumstances. The fear of change can hinder personal growth, limit opportunities, and perpetuate unhealthy patterns of thinking and behavior.

Mental fatigue is a state of cognitive exhaustion that can impair our ability to process information, make decisions, and engage in daily activities. This mind challenge can arise from prolonged periods of stress, lack of sleep, or an overload of information and stimuli. Mental fatigue can have significant consequences on our productivity, relationships, and overall well-being.

Psychological factors encompass the emotional, behavioral, and social aspects of our being that shape our thoughts, feelings, and actions. These factors can significantly influence our susceptibility to mind challenges and our ability to overcome them.

Emotional regulation refers to our ability to recognize, understand, and manage our emotions in a healthy and adaptive manner. Deficits in emotional regulation can contribute to the emergence of mind challenges, such as emotional roadblocks, impulsivity, and mood swings. By cultivating emotional intelligence and developing effective coping strategies, we can enhance our emotional regulation skills and better navigate the complexities of our emotional lives.

Self-esteem, the evaluation of our own worth and capabilities, plays a crucial role in our ability to face and overcome mind challenges. Low self-esteem can lead to self-doubt, indecision, and a lack of motivation, making it difficult to navigate the intricacies of decision-making and daily routines. By fostering self-compassion, self-acceptance, and self-efficacy, we can bolster our self-esteem and fortify our resilience against mind challenges.

Our social environment, including our relationships, cultural norms, and societal expectations, can significantly impact our susceptibility to mind challenges. Social influence can shape our beliefs, attitudes, and behaviors, either facilitating or hindering our ability to overcome cognitive obstacles. By cultivating supportive relationships, engaging in open dialogue, and challenging unhealthy social norms, we can mitigate the negative effects of social influence and foster a more conducive environment for personal growth.

Cognitive factors encompass the mental processes and structures that underlie our ability to perceive, process, and interpret information. These factors can significantly influence our vulnerability to mind challenges and our capacity to address them effectively.

Attention, the cognitive process responsible for selecting and focusing on relevant information, plays a crucial role in our ability to navigate mind challenges. Deficits in attention, such as those observed in multitasking or mental fatigue, can impair our ability to process information, make decisions, and engage in daily activities. By cultivating mindfulness, prioritizing tasks, and managing our cognitive resources, we can enhance our attentional capabilities and better navigate the complexities of our cognitive landscape.

Memory, the cognitive system responsible for encoding, storing, and retrieving information, can significantly influence our susceptibility to mind challenges. Factors such as memory biases, forgetting, and the misattribution of information can distort our perception of reality and hinder our ability to make informed decisions. By developing effective memory strategies, such as elaboration, organization, and rehearsal, we can enhance our mnemonic abilities and mitigate the impact of memory-related challenges.

Cognitive flexibility, the ability to adapt our thinking and behavior in response to changing circumstances, is a critical skill in navigating mind challenges. Deficits in cognitive flexibility, such as those observed in cognitive rigidity or the fear of change, can hinder our ability to adapt to new situations, learn from our experiences, and grow as individuals. By cultivating open-mindedness, curiosity, and a growth mindset, we can enhance our cognitive flexibility and better navigate the complexities of our ever-evolving cognitive landscape.

Executive functions, a set of high-level cognitive processes responsible for planning, organizing, and regulating our thoughts and actions, play a crucial role in our ability to navigate mind challenges. Deficits in executive functions, such as those observed in impulsivity, disorganization, or poor decision-making, can significantly impact our ability to process information, make decisions, and engage in daily activities. By developing effective executive function strategies, such as goal-setting, planning, and self-monitoring, we can enhance our cognitive control and better navigate the complexities of our cognitive landscape.

Decision-making, the cognitive process of selecting a course of action among multiple alternatives, is a fundamental aspect of human life. Mind challenges can significantly impair our ability to make informed and effective decisions, leading to a myriad of consequences.

Mind challenges can lead to indecision and analysis paralysis, where an individual becomes overwhelmed by the sheer volume of information and potential outcomes, resulting in an inability to make a decision. This can stem from fear of making the wrong choice, lack of self-confidence, or an inability to weigh the consequences of different options effectively. Indecision can result in missed opportunities, stagnation, and a sense of frustration and disempowerment.

Mind challenges can give rise to cognitive biases, systematic errors in thinking that can distort our perception of reality and influence our decision-making processes. These biases can arise from various sources, such as social, cultural, or personal factors, and can lead to flawed judgments and decisions. Examples of cognitive biases include confirmation bias, the tendency to seek out information that supports our preexisting beliefs while disregarding contradictory evidence, and the anchoring effect, the reliance on initial information when making subsequent judgments.

Mind challenges can also lead to an undue influence of emotions on our decision-making processes. Intense or unresolved emotions, such as fear, anger, or sadness, can hinder our ability to process information and make rational decisions. Emotional roadblocks can result in impulsive, irrational, or regretful choices that may not align with our long-term goals and values.

Our daily routines, the habits and activities that structure our lives, can also be significantly affected by mind challenges, leading to a range of consequences.

Mind challenges can manifest as procrastination, the act of delaying or postponing tasks, often leading to wasted time, increased stress, and a sense of unfulfillment. This can be driven by various factors, such as fear of failure, lack of motivation, or an inability to prioritize tasks effectively. Procrastination can have significant consequences on our productivity, relationships, and overall well-being.

The attempt to perform multiple tasks simultaneously, often referred to as multitasking, can be an outcome of mind challenges. While it may seem like an effective way to manage multiple responsibilities, research has shown that multitasking can actually impair our ability to focus and complete tasks efficiently. This can arise from an inability to prioritize tasks, a desire to accomplish more in less time, or a lack of self-discipline.

Perfectionism, the relentless pursuit of flawlessness, can be a manifestation of mind challenges. This can stem from high personal standards, a fear of failure, or a desire to gain approval from others. Perfectionism can lead to self-criticism, procrastination, and burnout, hindering our productivity and overall quality of life.

Mind challenges can also contribute to mental fatigue, a state of cognitive exhaustion that can impair our ability to process information, make decisions, and engage in daily activities. This can arise from prolonged periods of stress, lack of sleep, or an overload of information and stimuli. Mental fatigue can have significant consequences on our productivity, relationships, and overall well-being.

The ripple effect of mind challenges on decision-making and daily life is a complex and far-reaching phenomenon, with consequences that can significantly impact our mental, emotional, and social well-being. By understanding and addressing the intricate web of mind challenges, we can better navigate the complexities of our cognitive landscape, fostering self-awareness, resilience, and personal growth. In the face of adversity, let us embrace the beauty and complexity of the human psyche, forging ahead with courage and conviction in the pursuit of self-discovery and fulfillment.

Decision Paralysis and Effective Decision-Making Strategies

Every man carries a silent foe that haunts their thoughts. It hides in the shadows of hesitation, spreading its icy tendrils into our minds until we become immobilized. This intangible antagonist has no physical form, yet its power to undermine our will is formidable. It is decision paralysis - the inability to choose between options due to irrational fear, insecurity or confusion. And like any threat, it must be faced with courage if we hope to free ourselves from its grip.

There are times when the trivial matters of life seem fraught with uncertainties. A multitude of insignificant options can appear dizzyingly complex, foiling even our most mundane judgments. Should we wear the blue shirt or the gray? Eat at the diner down the street or try the new bistro? Small choices that really don't signify are blown up in our minds, as reason flees and frenzied self-doubt creeps in. We become paralyzed not because the decision truly has weighty consequences, but because we attach unnecessary importance to inconsequential things.

The root of decision paralysis often lies in our misguided need to always be right. We fret excessively over avoiding mistakes, real or imagined, that we lose sight of progress. But life rewards those who have learned to accept imperfection. No one bats a thousand, as the saying goes, yet we insist on putting unrealistic standards of perfection upon even our minor choices. If we hope to defeat paralysis, we must accept that all decisions will contain flaws and acknowledge that an imperfect decision today is better than no decision at all. The only true failure in life is standing still for fear of stumbling.

Procrastination, that familiar companion to indecision, only serves to amplify our doubts. We convince ourselves more time is needed to arrive at the perfect resolution, yet delay only breeds greater anxiety and fog. Standing frozen at the intersection of possibilities, we wander aimlessly down imaginary thoroughfares, going nowhere. But decisions, like time itself, will not wait. At some point, we must pick a path and step forward to see where it leads, learning from experience. To continue dawdling is to forfeit mastery over our fate. The remedy for hesitation is action.

For important choices that bear heavier stakes, resolving paralysis requires steeling our resolve. Visions of catastrophic outcomes have a way of disproportionately magnifying in our minds, yet such doomsday scenarios are rarely borne out in reality. We must distinguish between genuine risks and the exaggerated perils conjured by unrestrained "what ifs." It also helps to acknowledge that no decision will ever eliminate risk entirely; risk is part of life. If we place unrealistic expectations that a single judgment can guarantee perfect outcomes, we set ourselves up for chronic indecision. We all must find the courage to accept appropriate levels of risk if we want to grow beyond the safety of stasis.

A wise man once said that the difficult is what takes a little time, the impossible takes a little longer. Resolving complex dilemmas involving tough trade-offs may necessitate more careful consideration. Yet procrastination is still the enemy. Speaking with others, gathering diverse perspectives, weighing pros and cons - such steps can bring much-needed clarity. Ultimately though, all facts will never be on the table. At a certain point, we must trust our judgment even when uncertain. To act is brave, to delay is to relinquish control. Though the future is not ours to see, choicelessness ensures a future led by doubt rather than direction.

Many find their confidence sapped by fear of failure or disapproval from others. But we will never please all people, and a perfect solution sits beyond reach. We must be willing to risk disappointing some and make peace with the likelihood of mistakes. Recognize too that the tangible consequences of failure are usually not as bad as imagined. And should things indeed go wrong, have faith in your ability to learn from experience. Defeat paralysis by accepting you cannot control outcomes, only your decision to act despite the unknown. You have but this moment; do not squander it too timid to trust yourself.

Habit is also an enemy that sneaks up unnoticed. Routines, no matter how unproductive, become instinct if not regularly challenged. Complacency breeds inaction, and inertia grows where initiative once flourished. To defeat lifelong paralysis, we must develop the discipline to regularly question routines and conventions that once served but now only imprison. New perspectives and experiences outside our comfort zone can recharge stale thinking. And in times of persistent doubt, seeking contrasting views from unusual allies may surprise us with a fresh angle before. Complacency is the slow death of potential; keep evolving.

Ultimately, what separates those able to act from those paralyzed by angst is willingness to acknowledge uncertainty and discomfort as natural parts of life. Mistakes, risks and doubts - we all must face these companions if we hope to journey beyond the familiar. The rewards of progression far outweigh clinging to stasis out of fear. So understand decision paralysis as a test of courage rather than intellect. Have faith that you have the grit within to get through difficult patches by keeping eyes focused ahead rather than fixated on potential stumbles. There are always unknowns, but you need not let them define you. Now go - the day awaits your choice.

Decision paralysis arises when we place unrealistic expectations upon ourselves that a single choice can guarantee perfect outcomes with zero risk of mistakes or failure. But life presents no such guarantee. We all must develop the courage to accept appropriate levels of risk, learn from experience despite imperfections, and trust our judgment - even when uncertain - if we want to break free from the immobilizing grip of indecision. Have faith in your ability to adapt despite unknowable challenges ahead. If we regularly question routines, seek alternate views, and accept discomfort as natural, we strengthen our resolve to face life's silent enemies within. Now it is time to make enemies of doubt and choose action. Your future is forged not by fate but by your decisions today.

All journeys, no matter the distance, must begin with a single step. Yet how does one take the first stride when faced with a dilemna as treacherous and convoluted as a swamp - sucking one down into an abyss of endless variables and obscure pathways? When a decision has spawned so many intersecting tangles that the whole situation seems an impassible morass, how does one go about cutting through the quicksand to actually initiate progress?

The first tactic is realizing that complexity itself is truly a mirage. No problem, however knotted its outward form, is impenetrable at its core. With steady analysis and sheer grit, any encumbrance can be broken down into more manageable component pieces. One need only have the discipline and fortitude to slowly peel away distracting externals, getting to the bare essentials of what really matters. With persistence, any Gordian knot can be untied strand by strand rather than foolishly attacking it as one indigestible mass.

Start by taking a step back to gain a bird's-eye view of the landscape. Get some physical distance and look at the bigger picture from a new vantage point, literally or figuratively. Often what seemed a hopeless tangle of minutiae up close reveals itself as belonging to recognizable patterns and classifications once one can see the wider context and terrain. Major themes and priorities tend to emerge clearly from a broader outlook, allowing the extraneous clutter to fall away naturally.

Once the essential topography is visible, it's time to pull out the machete and start methodically chopping down unmanageable thickets into navigable segments. But do not take on more than can be reasonably handled at a time. Break the mass problem down into its most basic constituent pieces - no more than five to seven discrete components is the normally optimum number for the human mind to juggle meaningfully. Resist the urge to preserve the illusion of singularity and instead cut straight through to reality's articulated parts.

Prioritize according to significance and dependencies. Some sections clearly form the foundation upon which others are built, so address these preliminary matters first. Leave room for iterative adjustments as understanding deepens and priorities may shift in focus with new information or changing circumstances. Build in flexibility to weave back together alignments that evolve rather than insisting on rigid uniformity from the start. Solutions often emerge organically through patience and willingness to rework divisions in response to ongoing insights.

Work through parts sequentially while maintaining clear sight of the end goal. Tackle one comprehensible component after another, making sure each advance takes you closer to the ultimate objective before moving to new terrains. Periodically step back again to confirm alignment of mini-journeys with the overarching purpose, adjusting routes that appear to stray off course. Stay accountable by tracking performance against benchmarks and deadlines to sustain momentum despite inevitable setbacks along the way.

As logical and simplified as this linear manner may seem, life has an impish way of springing asymmetrical patterns from even our best-laid plans. Be ready to take the occasional meandering or diversive detour if valuable intelligence promises to significantly illuminate or refine the core issues at play. Indeed, some of the richest veins of understanding may originate from information apparently extraneous to stated goals but meriting a brief exploration nonetheless. Trust your intuition as much as logic when nosing out insights that could provide transformative surprises.

At the same time, set clear time limits on tangents so divergences don't balloon out of control and lose focus of the main objectives. Have discipline to pull thoughts back on track before drifting irretrievably astray. Not all that glitters will prove golden; learn to leave some intriguing but marginal leads fallow if they threaten to filch attention from your basic purposes.

Boundless curiosity alone will assuredly strand one chin-deep in triviality's bogs forevermore.

Perhaps counterintuitively, seek perspectives beyond usual confines when tackling hairy complexities. Insouciant or tangential thinker allies can lend keen vision by dint of very unfamiliarity with dogmatic conventions or customary mindsets. Their alien vantage liberates them to connect dots unseen by those whose ingrained assumptions form blinkers. A divergent thinker's maverick hypothesis might just illuminate the key to breakthrough. At minimum, exposing foundations to scrutiny by skeptical outsiders usefully tests vulnerabilities and expands the field of possibilities considered.

Constantly question, challenge and reconstruct all premises as work progresses. Subject every aspect, however fundamental it first appears, to a willing posture of revision in light of accumulating evidence and new links drawn between matters. Organic problems demand organic solutions adaptable to morphing realities, not rigid schemas naively presumed immutable. True progress occurs at the boundaries and intersections where disparate ways of knowing intersectively stimulate innovative syntheses from apparent contradictions.

Ultimately, what seems an intractable swamp of complexity conceals a hidden gift - the opportunity to strengthen resourcefulness through grappling with limitations. Tackling an immense, convoluted issue a bite-sized chunk at a time trains us in focusing concentration amid welter. Breaking free of perceived restraints builds confidence and mastery over circumstances we previously imagined controlling us. Each small victory encourages, reminding that steady persistence will overcome the most daunting of obstacles given ongoing commitment. Most of all, simplifying an overwhelming multifaceted dilemma trains the mind in distilling essence from appearance - a wisdom serving well in all life's tangled and transformative passages.

Complexity poses a challenge we must meet resolutely with patience, tenacity and open-mindedness. By taking a broader view, sectioning immense issues into discrete segments, prioritizing logically whilst maintaining flexibility, plus subjecting all assumptions to scrutiny - immense dilemmas can be broken into portions bite-sized enough for progress. Realizing that convolutions conceal actual simplicity empowers us to cut through obfuscation strategically using intellect and the invaluable asset of experience itself. Ultimately, tackling life's toughest knotted problems is less about concocting infallible masterplans, more about cultivating the grit, guile and willingness to learn demanded by everyday realities. With commitment, any riddle however tangled begins yielding its secrets.

The open road beckons with possibilities, yet where does it truly lead without guidance? Wander as we may, chance alone will not deliver us from doubt to resolution. To transform confusion into clarity and inaction into forward motion, we must actively seek understanding from many sources – but not to the point of paralysis. In times that try men's souls with perplexing crossroads, inner stillness shows the way through gathering diverse counsel, setting boundary markers on rumination, and trusting intuition born of preparation to propel us beyond hesitation at last.

Information is the ballast that steadies determination against shifting tides. Facts anchor vision to realities beyond subjective fears alone. But gather knowledge we must through varied avenues, questioning all we assume to know with an open yet discerning mind. Personal biases hold fast unless loosened by considering alternate lenses on circumstances. Expert voices offer experience yet lack fulsome context; outsider perspectives challenge limitations and expand horizons. No single resource supplies the entire picture – truth emerges by gathering mosaic fragments from diverse provenances into a multifaceted whole.

Make a careful study of all angles through diligent inquiry from experts as well as those nearer hearth and field. Keep an open receptiveness to new frames yet guard against distraction by trivial matters or opinions based more in sentiment than observation and reason. Let merits decide which accounts carry weight, recognizing that definitive certainties are fleeting but reasoned likelihoods suffice. One truth serves many functions; gather what matters pragmatically to inform workable options without becoming mired by perfectionism or superfluity.

Information alone, however, is but dry kindling. Instinct sparks purpose when facts combust in the crucible of intuition. Headlong into thickets on passion or whim risks losing direction, but timidity ensures stagnation. The middle way between extremes channels rationality and feeling toward clarity. Get traction from fundamentals while permitting room for hunches born of unconscious patterns and life's lessons thus far. Inner promptings deserve respect as messengers from experience digesting details below surface sight. Let instinct steers facts toward significance recognizable to your core values and strengths.

Trust that deeper instincts align with your authentic self over time through making, learning from mistakes. Confidence emerges from repeatedly validating gut promptings against outcomes. However, leave openings for adapting as changing times surface new nuances. Flexibility of spirit preserves relevance along life's winding paths. Open but discerning examination of root causes refines instinct's compass against off-course diversions rationalized by wish or fear alone. Facts ground vision, instinct provides direction – together they form a surer foundation than either could alone.

Yet even united vision and purpose need walls to build momentum vital for crossing undefined terrain. Deadlines delineate initiatives from stagnating deliberation. Without markers to drive progress against indecision's sands, even the clearest objectives risk foundering. Install waystations to check alignment and pace, leaving space for adaptation yet holding firm where procrastination threatens forward motion. Measure attainable targets realistically but in a manner demanding consistent effort, recalibrating if initial aims prove misaligned or conditions shift demands.

Respect due dates as contracts with self as much as external considerations. Meeting goals on time reinforces discipline and trust in one's abilities. Slippage erodes assurance if indulged without accountability. At the same time, rigid dogmatism leads nowhere - course corrections sometimes require pausing to rediscover bearings rather than stubbornly diving ahead. Instinct and facts must harmonize daily to avoid missing larger opportunities awaiting those nimble enough to spot open windows amid change's winds. Flexibility serves consistency when employed strategically rather than as license for empty drift.

Most of all, learn to accept uncertainty as life's permanent condition rather than illusion of its absence compelling paralysis or rushed decisions. Not knowing every particular ahead makes a hash of even best-laid plans at times - expect bumps, adapt through them. Inner strength endures uncertain terrain by focusing steadfastly on progress fueled by dedication to growth through challenge rather than arrival at some final destination. Purpose derives from journey, not singular resolutions - so keep moving mindfully through shifting reality toward aspirations undimmed by circumstance. Our days are lent, not given; use time well yet lightly, without grasping at assurances beyond human reach or control.

Faith in one's ability to navigate ambiguity through diligent yet open-hearted effort allows transformation of hardship into opportunity. Facts, instinct, boundaries – these pillars support empowered choice when uncertainty most besets. But only by accepting life's changing currents can we overcome fear of the unknowable to steer purposefully through both calms and storms. The road calls all travelers finally to let go clinging and continue the pilgrimage with courage, grace and trust that each step further unravels what mysteries truly signify along humanity's wayfaring.

Making headway amid complexity demands we anchor uncertainty with multiple perspectives yet guard against analysis paralysis through setting healthy limits. Facts provide ballast, intuition direction - but it is deadlines alone ensuring progress while allowing adaptation. Rigidity finds no destinations, flexibility has no departure; the middle path embraces learning through commitment amid inevitable surprises. Most of all, recognizing perils emerge from grasping rather than conditions permits transforming even confusion's swamps into solid footing by keeping focused upward and outward, come what may. Our days are lent - use them well.

Gathering information is a critical step in the decision-making process, as it provides the foundation upon which we base our choices. The importance of gathering information can be attributed to several key factors:

Enhanced Understanding: Gathering information enables us to develop a deeper understanding of the situation, the available options, and the potential consequences of our choices. This enhanced understanding allows us to make more informed and confident decisions.

Reduced Uncertainty: Information gathering helps to reduce uncertainty by providing insights into the various factors that may influence the outcome of our decisions. By reducing uncertainty, we can make decisions with greater clarity and assurance.

Risk Mitigation: Gathering information allows us to identify and assess potential risks associated with each option, enabling us to make decisions that minimize risk and maximize potential benefits.

Improved Predictability: Information gathering can help us to better predict the outcomes of our decisions, allowing us to make choices that are more likely to result in our desired results.

To optimize the decision-making process, it's essential to employ effective information-gathering strategies. Some of these strategies include:

Diversify Information Sources: To gain a comprehensive understanding of the situation, it's important to gather information from a variety of sources. This can include expert opinions, research studies, news articles, and personal experiences.

Evaluate Information Quality: Not all information is created equal, and it's crucial to critically evaluate the quality and reliability of the information we gather. This can involve assessing the credibility of sources, checking for biases, and verifying information through multiple sources.

Ask the Right Questions: To gather relevant and useful information, it's important to ask the right questions. This can involve clarifying our objectives, identifying key stakeholders, and considering potential challenges and opportunities.

Setting time limits is another crucial aspect of the decision-making process, as it helps to ensure that decisions are made in a timely and efficient manner. The importance of setting time limits can be attributed to several key factors:

Preventing Analysis Paralysis: Setting time limits can help to prevent analysis paralysis, a situation in which an individual becomes overwhelmed by the sheer volume of information and potential outcomes, resulting in an inability to make a decision.

Encouraging Action: Time limits can provide a sense of urgency and motivation, encouraging us to take action and make decisions in a timely manner.

Enhancing Efficiency: Setting time limits can help to streamline the decision-making process, ensuring that we allocate our time and resources effectively and efficiently.

Promoting Accountability: Time limits can promote accountability, as they encourage us to take responsibility for our decisions and their outcomes.

To optimize the decision-making process, it's essential to employ effective time limit-setting strategies. Some of these strategies include:

Prioritize Decisions: To allocate time effectively, it's important to prioritize decisions based on their urgency, importance, and potential impact. This can involve creating a decision-making hierarchy or using a decision matrix to weigh the pros and cons of each option.

Establish Realistic Deadlines: Setting realistic deadlines is crucial for ensuring that decisions are made in a timely manner without compromising the quality of the decision-making process. This can involve considering the complexity of the decision, the availability of information, and the potential consequences of the decision.

Break Down Complex Decisions: For complex decisions, it can be helpful to break the decision-making process into smaller, more manageable steps, each with its own time limit. This can help to simplify the process and ensure that each aspect of the decision is given the appropriate attention.

The art of decision-making is a complex and multifaceted process, requiring careful consideration, information gathering, and time management. By understanding the importance of gathering information and setting time limits for decision-making, we can optimize our decision-making processes, making more informed, confident, and effective choices. As we navigate the intricate landscape of decision-making, let us embrace the power of knowledge and the value of time, forging ahead with courage and conviction in the pursuit of wisdom and growth.

Procrastination and Boosting Productivity

Each new day dawns aglow with promise, unsullied by the dusts of yesterday. Yet for some, dawn elicits not eager hands seizing opportunity but fists clenched tight to ward off obligations creeping ever closer. Where ambition once flourished now lingers only inertia, as doubts insinuate reasons to delay the inevitable a while longer. Procrastination, subtle thief of potential, creeps among us disguised as friend - but its affections come at a crippling cost if followed down fruitless byways. To conquer this shape-shifting scourge demands facing its moldering roots and fortifying purpose against future inroads.

At procrastination's core often lurks fear - whether of inadequacy, judgment, or life's flux itself. Where uncertainty reigns, paralysis besets the timid. But few situations present all factors clearly. Accepting enigma as reality's fabric is healthier than hoping resolution through avoidance alone. Grow by shouldering uncertainty, not shrinking from its mere presence. Faith in one's mettle outlasts circumstance; deny fears domination and see they shelter weakness, not spare it. Courage meets each challenge, however veiled, with eyes open rather than fleeing behind willful ignorance.

For others, inertia may spring more from warped views of consequence. Mountains imagined from molehills distort perspective, inflating trivial tasks till Herculean. But accomplishments rarely match dreams of perfection, and completion itself rewards where fantasies only exhaust. Break projects into bite-sized, achievable increments; track progress toward destinations visible if distantly, not consumed by each foothill obscuring the path ahead. Realize also that no duty is so critical as to justify lost chances - delays diminish opportunities unfolding elsewhere amid life's transitions.

At times, rootlessness itself energizes delay, as perpetual searching masks indecision. But life grants no reprieve from choosing; recognize evasion for what it is and embrace challenges howsoever unplanned as vehicles instead of voids. Duty is opportunity in disguise for those willing to commit hands to plow unsentimentally. Discover direction through doing, not fantasizing; stay grounded by keeping dreams tightly leashed to diligent effort, lest they go feral and mislead. Focus outward and just begin - one step enough to spark momentum where doubt once reigned.

Inertia may arise too from imbalance - when relaxations outpace exertion in a lifestyle of all rest, no work. But moderation, not excess, provides sanctuary from life's buffets. Work sharpened by play maintains zest where grindstone routines blunt purpose. Monitor priorities closely lest recreations commandeer existence; nourish spirit through balanced intake, not gluttony alone. Learn too that diversions become purpose in their way - seek fulfillment through varied calls upon your time and talents, not escape alone. Activity refreshes where stagnation stifles; find equilibrium sustaining motivation.

Procrastination thrives also on baser impulses. Instant pleasures tempt some from prolonged labors yielding rewards invisible beside pressing whims. Yet discipline – not severity but adherence to priorities polished smooth through practice

– holds back shortsighted passions from dominating paths forward. Learn delayed gratification through substituting immediate desires occasional with commitments enriching over time. Balance indulgence with investment in your potential and see gains compound beyond momentary highs alone. With perseverance comes sustaining fulfillment far outstripping fleeting excitation.

While fears, beliefs and habits provide kindling, distraction most fans procrastination's smoldering to active blaze. In networking age, information overload and constant stimulation drain focus available for commitments. Monitor data deluges and limit non-essential interruption; carve dedicated times free from distraction for concentrating effort. Learn also to say no to peripheral attractions drawing attention from obligations. Assertiveness, not avoidance, tackles life's multidimensional demands with intention guiding allocation of precious minutes.

The costs of lost time mount swiftly. Projects stall, opportunities wither, goals remain distant shadows of intention. But far worse, chronic avoidance habits erode self-belief. Failures result less from ineptitude than paralysis of analysis. Regain assurance through insisting small daily victories dismantle lethargy's defenses piece by piece. Forgive setbacks without self-castigation; perseverance transforms all obstacles given open and optimistic spirit. Monitor slippage carefully to catch inertia's seeds before sprouting, yet greet failures as lessons rather than condemnation if persistence followed. Strength emerges through adversity met squarely with grit, not overcome through denial of life's difficulties. There, procrastination's mastery exists.

Procrastination springs from fixable roots when traced - fears, perspectives and habits demanding adjustment not avoidance. Its consequences devastate potential through diminishing not only accomplishments but self-belief itself over time. Yet all threats contain within seeds of remedies also, if gathered with clear-eyed tenacity. Understanding procrastination's causes empowers shifting motivations outward through undertaking however small each day's task brought near through discipline, and greeting outcomes - whatever face presented - with eyes ahead rather than down. Growth originates at edges of comfort, not within; rise to each challenge with open hand and heart, let come what may. Tomorrow waits on intentions made substance by dedicated actions - not dreams alone - today.

Each new day presents possibilities as boundless as the horizon, yet how does one cut through potential's fog to shape intangible yearnings into something concrete enough to propel determined effort? Vision alone sustains few for long without stakes in the nearer ground of achievable purpose. To transform abstraction into forward motion demands focusing dreams through the sharpening lens of discipline - setting goals anchored firmly in reality, then prioritizing tasks to transform objectives step by step from idea to incarnation. Here are some practical techniques for making progress tangible.

Begin by anchoring aspirations tightly to honest self-assessment. Know strengths, weaknesses, limits - do not inflate abilities or underestimate demands. Be candid yet optimistic, distinguishing wants from realistic capacities given resources and responsibilities. Consult outside views too, without bias; others see blind spots invisible to our emotional investment. Let temper passions with pragmatism, distinguishing practical potentials from frivolous fantasies through dispassionate contemplation. When horizons align with capabilities, grounds for success take root.

Establish goals specific, measurable and timely. Avoid ambiguous declarations impervious to tracking. Go granular to maintain perspective on progress versus perfectionism. Assign quantifiers wherever possible - numbers reached, tasks completed, savings accrued. Attach realistic completion dates factoring contingencies to translate possibilities into schedule. Measurability and deadline accountability strengthen willpower where ethereal visions dissolve effort.

Make objectives demanding without exceeding limits. Overly modest aims surrender to inertia; excessively lofty ones breed discouragement. Reach by progressively stretching, not strangling possibility. Build in room for small wins maintaining momentum against obstacles while avoiding frustration from oversized bites. Periodically review and consciously recalibrate rising and falling targets in response to evolving strengths, conditions and insights gained along the way. Flexibility preserves relevance better than rigidity.

Prioritize ruthlessly based on significance and dependencies. Ascertain which goals form foundations others rely on; address these first to enable subsequent progress. Clarify how achievements build upon each other, sequencing tasks logically. Be willing to delay peripherals that distract from weightier missions driving you forward most directly. Learn to leave some desires fallow if tangential versus serving overarching purposes. Concentration of effort multiplies returns where scattered energy achieves little.

Realize too that life presents divergences demanding balance away from dedicated pursuits. Monitor priorities lest obligations encroach health or relationships. Safeguard fundamental values like community, character, experience alongside productivity. Growth originates through varied challenges; diversity maintains well-being and perspective refreshing where monomania burns brightest but briefly. Learn from history's driven whose inflexibility undermined larger causes for transient victories achieved at life's expense alone. Equilibrium sustains where imbalance steals from soul the nourishment fueling tenacity through challenges ahead.

Break projects down into actionable next steps however small, allocating daily increments toward completion. Visualize progress regularly through checkpoints and concrete behaviors changing as goals near. Transforming nebulous future into clear schedule strengthens willpower against ambivalence. But learn too to accept and adapt periodically to deviations inevitably encountered amid life's flux. Flexibility of spirit maintains relevance where rigidity ensures failure against realities beyond perfect ordering. Have faith that patience and persistence bear fruit despite surprises inevitably scattered along the path.

Learn from history, yet chart your own course informed by introspection alone. No one destination suits all; what inspires some leaves others cold. Find within your authentic motivations; do not run roads walked by others without considering your needs. Confidence arises from ownership of aims consistent with your gifting, temperament and priorities. Achievements ring hollow mimicking foreign blueprints versus pursuits in harmony with your heart's song. Let vision form through self-inquiry rather than preconceptions; rise to possibilities made substance through your dedicated actions.

Goal-setting succeeds most through steady refinement versus arrival at final formulations. Progress emerges through translating shifting currents encountered daily into forward motion rather than chasing fixed endpoints. Flexibility, balance and willingness to continually learn from experience - these sustain where rigidity ensures stagnation. Most of all, remember each small consistency widening the scope of possible through diligence widens further still your understanding of potential within. Stay dedicated to growth through journey more than singular destinations; destinations change, but improvement remains eternal through open and persevering spirit. Now, go - opportunities await the hands readied to receive them.

Goal-setting holds the key to transforming drifting vision into purposeful forward motion - when anchored firmly in self-awareness, pursued incrementally through prioritizing significance, yet balanced adaptively amid life's realities. Progress occurs through committed action, not fantasies alone; track concrete objectives, behaviors and milestones to convert intangible aspirations step-by-step into enduring results. Most of all, focus outward through consistently applying lessons learned each day rather than fixating on final endpoints. Mastery exists not in preconceptions, but in ongoing translation of experiences into ever-widening possibilities realized through dedicated next steps. Now, onward - the journey awaits.

While dreams stir restless spirit, realities of limitation curb even the sturdiest wills without pragmatic ordering of priorities. Time marches on indifferent to human schemes; to seize control of its slipping currency requires maintaining presence amid distractions, focusing energy on pursuits bearing fruit, and finding anchor in community upholding purpose where lone efforts falter. Here are strategies for not only maximizing minutes, but sustaining commitment through fellowship.

Begin each cycle consciously aligning activities to core values and objectives. avoid drifting upon tides of whimsy; stay rooted through visualizing impact of each task. Discern significance to avoid trivialities leeching hours better spent.

Impose regimen without rigidity; structure provides framework for exploiting fleeting moments rather than anxiety. Monitor alignment regularly; flexibility maintains freshness where rigidity courts failure against life's flux. Focus energizes where scatter dissipates potential.

Prioritize ruthlessly. Triage according to consequence, dependencies, urgency rather than preference. Leave desires fallow that undermine weightier targets. Concentrate might where it drives progress furthest. Yet judge potential in tasks too, not completion alone - small gestures compound impact over time. Avoid "just get it done" mindsets substituting activeness for actual productivity. Let intrinsic reward through challenge entice, not deadline stress alone. Health demands balance, so safeguard reasonable reserves from overcommitting though discipline.

Chunk projects into bite-sized actions. Large objectives paralyze; decompose into incremental steps visibly increasing chance of success daily. Visualize progress concretely to bolster perseverance against difficulty. Set deadlines realistically yet demandingly; consistency transforms obstacles, not perfection alone. Measure improvements regularly to recalibrate schedule amid life's turns. Flexibility harmonizes with purpose better than rigidity against reality's variables.

Learn to say no. Guard energies from peripheral distractions diluting focus. Master communication economizing transaction costs otherwise siphoning hours. Prior experience helps navigate complexity's thickets gracefully through intuition honed by practice more than exhaustive planning alone. Automate routines; habit promotes ease, freeing attention for tasks demanding spontaneity. Yet resist complete systematizing too; balance structure with improvisation sustaining edge and enjoyment where predictability flattens spirit.

Accountability multiplies effort through presence beyond lone vigils. Find allies energizing purpose where solitary dedication risks flagging. Share burdens buoying each other through difficulty. Healthy competition lights fires; learn also cooperative spirit magnifying individual capacities. Fellowship sustains where ambitions risk turning inward and dissipating against life's demands. Shared commitment holds members to highest standards while embracing shared humanity. Community transforms effort from chore into source of profound connection and growth beyond any single person's scope.

Time management like any discipline succeeds through balance - structure focusing potential yet flexibility adapting relevance amid life's flux, priorities ruthlessly aligning tasks to purpose yet space for intuition and relationships guarding impact from turning myopic or brittle. Progress originates at edges where newness stimulates; stay ever evolving through open yet discerning spirit. Most of all, remember hours present but moments in service of larger causes and connections elevating daily toils beyond temporal transitory concerns alone. Now, go - opportunities await the hands readied to receive their gifts through diligence and fellowship both.

Maximizing fleeting moments demands aligning activities to core values through routine yet preparedness for life's surprises. Focus and prioritization concentrate potential where scatter dissipates impact. Chunking projects and setting deadlines sustain momentum, while accountability through community uplifts efforts beyond any lone capacity. Ultimately, mastery exists not in rigidity but balance - focusing energy yet maintaining flexibility and presence beyond self alone through relationships nourishing purpose eternally beyond temporal limitations. Now, the day presents its offerings; go transform hours into contributions through discipline and fellowship both.

Information Overload and Enhancing Focus

In today's fast-paced and interconnected world, individuals are constantly bombarded with vast amounts of information from various sources. This phenomenon, known as information overload, can have significant effects on decision-making and daily routines.

Information overload refers to the state in which individuals are exposed to an excessive amount of information, making it difficult to process, analyze, and make informed decisions. The proliferation of digital technologies, social media, and the internet has exacerbated this issue, as information is now more accessible and abundant than ever before.

Several factors contribute to information overload, including:

The rapid growth of digital technologies: The exponential growth of digital technologies has led to an explosion of information, making it challenging for individuals to keep up with the constant influx of data.

The need for instant gratification: The desire for immediate access to information has led to a culture of constant connectivity, where individuals feel compelled to check their devices frequently for updates and notifications.

The fear of missing out (FOMO): The fear of missing out on important information or events can drive individuals to seek out and consume more information than they can reasonably process.

The pressure to stay informed: In today's competitive and fast-paced environment, individuals often feel pressured to stay informed about a wide range of topics, leading to information overload.

Information overload can have significant consequences on decision-making, including:

Analysis paralysis: The abundance of information can lead to analysis paralysis, a state in which individuals are unable to make decisions due to the overwhelming number of options and factors to consider.

Decreased decision quality: Information overload can result in hasty or suboptimal decisions, as individuals may not have the cognitive capacity to process and analyze all the available information thoroughly.

Increased stress and anxiety: The pressure to process and make decisions based on vast amounts of information can lead to increased stress and anxiety, negatively impacting mental health and well-being.

Information overload can also have significant consequences on daily routines, including:

Reduced productivity: The constant influx of information can lead to frequent interruptions and distractions, making it difficult for individuals to focus on tasks and complete them efficiently.

Impaired time management: Information overload can make it challenging for individuals to prioritize tasks and allocate their time effectively, leading to procrastination and missed deadlines.

Diminished work-life balance: The need to stay constantly connected and informed can blur the boundaries between work and personal life, leading to an unhealthy work-life balance and increased stress.

To mitigate the effects of information overload on decision-making and daily routines, individuals can employ several strategies, including:

Setting boundaries: Establishing clear boundaries around information consumption, such as designating specific times for checking emails and social media, can help individuals manage the influx of information and maintain focus on their tasks.

Prioritizing information: Individuals should prioritize the information they consume based on its relevance and importance to their goals and objectives.

Simplifying decision-making: Simplifying decision-making processes, such as by breaking down complex decisions into smaller, more manageable steps, can help individuals overcome analysis paralysis and make better decisions.

Developing mindfulness: Cultivating mindfulness and self-awareness can help individuals recognize when they are experiencing information overload and take appropriate steps to manage it.

Methods for Limiting Exposure to Distractions

Establish a designated workspace: Creating a dedicated workspace free from distractions can significantly improve focus and productivity. This space should be comfortable, well-lit, and equipped with the necessary tools and resources for the task at hand.

Set clear boundaries: Establishing clear boundaries between work and personal life is essential for maintaining focus. This may involve setting specific work hours, turning off notifications during focused work periods, and communicating your availability to friends, family, and colleagues.

Implement time management techniques: Time management techniques, such as the Pomodoro Technique or time blocking, can help individuals structure their time more effectively and minimize distractions. These methods involve breaking work into focused intervals, followed by short breaks to recharge and refocus.

Practice mindfulness and self-awareness: Developing mindfulness and self-awareness can help individuals recognize when they are becoming distracted and take appropriate steps to refocus their attention. This may involve meditation, deep breathing exercises, or simply taking a brief walk to clear the mind.

Utilize technology wisely: While technology can be a significant source of distraction, it can also be a valuable tool for limiting exposure to distractions. Apps and software that block distracting websites, silence notifications, or help manage tasks can be invaluable for maintaining focus and productivity.

Methods for Organizing Information Effectively

Create a system for organizing information: Developing a consistent system for organizing information, such as filing, labeling, or categorizing, can help individuals to quickly and easily access the information they need when they need it.

Prioritize information: Prioritizing information based on its relevance and importance can help individuals to focus on the most critical tasks and information, reducing the risk of becoming overwhelmed by less important details.

Utilize visual aids: Visual aids, such as mind maps, flowcharts, or diagrams, can help individuals to organize and process complex information more effectively. These tools can help to identify patterns, connections, and relationships between different pieces of information, facilitating better understanding and decision-making.

Employ note-taking strategies: Effective note-taking strategies, such as the Cornell Method or the Outline Method, can help individuals to organize and process information more efficiently. These strategies involve summarizing, paraphrasing, and categorizing information in a structured format, making it easier to review and recall later.

Leverage technology for information management: Technology can be a powerful tool for organizing and managing information. Utilizing project management software, digital note-taking apps, or cloud storage solutions can help individuals to keep their information organized, accessible, and up-to-date.

Exploring mindfulness techniques, such as meditation, can greatly enhance our ability to focus and make decisions in our daily lives. The practice of mindfulness involves being fully present and aware of our thoughts, feelings, and surroundings without judgment. By cultivating a sense of mindfulness, we can overcome the various challenges that may arise when making decisions or navigating through our daily routines.

One common challenge that many individuals face when making decisions is indecision or analysis paralysis. This occurs when we are unable to make a decision due to feeling overwhelmed by the number of options available or fearing making the wrong choice. In order to overcome this challenge, practicing mindfulness techniques such as meditation can help quiet the mind and cultivate a sense of clarity and focus. By grounding ourselves in the present moment, we can more easily assess our options and make decisions that align with our values and goals.

Another challenge that may arise when making decisions is emotional reactivity. This occurs when our emotions cloud our judgment and prevent us from making rational decisions. Mindfulness techniques such as meditation can help us cultivate emotional intelligence and self-awareness, allowing us to better regulate our emotions and make decisions from a place of calmness and clarity. By observing our thoughts and emotions without attachment, we can gain a greater sense of control over our decision-making process.

Furthermore, mindfulness techniques can help improve our ability to focus and concentrate on the task at hand. In today's fast-paced world, we are constantly bombarded with distractions that can hinder our ability to make decisions effectively. By practicing mindfulness techniques such as meditation, we can train our minds to stay present and focused, allowing us to make decisions with greater clarity and intention.

Emotional Roadblocks and Building Emotional Resilience

The impact of powerful emotions cannot be undermined. Emotions, those indomitable currents that surge through our consciousness, possess the potential to shape our judgments and guide our choices.

Emotions, those intangible forces that color our existence, possess a remarkable ability to influence the human mind in myriad ways. From elation to despair, from ecstasy to anger, emotions can act as persuasive whispers or deafening roars, shaping our perception of reality and molding our choices. The impact of strong emotions on decision-making lies in their capacity to alter our cognitive processes, coloring our judgment and steering us towards certain courses of action.

When emotions run high, they have the power to skew our perceptions, leading us down paths that may deviate from rationality. This cognitive landscape, fraught with biases, can be a treacherous terrain for those seeking objective decision-making. One such bias is the confirmation bias, where individuals selectively seek out information that aligns with their emotions, reinforcing preconceived notions and inhibiting a comprehensive analysis of the situation. Moreover, emotions can engender a heightened susceptibility to the framing effect, where the presentation of information or options can significantly impact our choices. We become vulnerable to manipulation, as emotions cloud our ability to critically evaluate the information at hand, leading to suboptimal decisions.

Neuroscience provides us with a glimpse into the intricate dance between emotions and decision-making that unfolds within the recesses of our brains. When emotions surge, the amygdala, that ancient sentinel of the mind, takes center stage, signaling the presence of potential threats or rewards. This activation of the amygdala can hijack the decision-making process, diminishing the role of rational thought and propelling us towards impulsive actions. Simultaneously, the prefrontal cortex, the seat of logical reasoning, often finds itself engaged in a power struggle with the emotional centers of the brain. This tussle between reason and emotion further complicates the decision-making process, as we attempt to strike a delicate balance between the two.

While the influence of strong emotions on decision-making is undeniable, it is crucial to recognize that emotions can be both friend and foe. They can serve as beacons of intuition, guiding us towards choices that align with our deepest desires and values.

Passionate emotions can fuel innovation, drive, and determination, propelling us towards audacious goals. However, without careful introspection and self-awareness, emotions can also cloud our judgment, leading to impulsive and regrettable decisions. It is in understanding the duality of emotions that we can harness their power to our advantage.

Given the intricate interplay between emotions and decision-making, it becomes imperative to explore strategies that can mitigate the potential negative effects. Developing emotional intelligence, the ability to recognize, understand, and manage emotions, can foster self-awareness and enable us to navigate the complex terrain of decision-making more effectively. Additionally, seeking diverse perspectives and soliciting feedback can help counteract the confirmation bias, providing a more holistic view of the situation at hand. Mindfulness practices, such as meditation, can also cultivate a state of heightened awareness, allowing us to observe our emotions without being consumed by them. By incorporating these strategies into our decision-making processes, we can strive for more balanced and objective judgments.

The impact of strong emotions on judgment and decision-making is a multifaceted phenomenon that lies at the intersection of psychology, neuroscience, and human experience. Emotions possess an undeniable power to shape our perceptions, biases, and choices. While they can serve as potent catalysts for both positive and negative outcomes, it is crucial to approach decision-making with awareness and discernment. By understanding the intricate interplay between emotions and cognition, we can navigate the labyrinthine corridors of our minds with greater clarity, making decisions that align with our values and aspirations. As the tapestry of emotions weaves its intricate patterns, let us strive to unravel its mysteries and forge a path towards wiser and more informed decision-making.

Self-awareness, that profound state of consciousness wherein we become cognizant of our own thoughts, emotions, and motivations, serves as a beacon of enlightenment.Introduction

In the realm of decision-making, the significance of self-awareness and self-reflection cannot be underestimated. To truly comprehend the depths of this crucial facet, one must embark on a journey of introspection, unraveling the enigmatic layers of the human psyche.

Self-awareness, that profound state of consciousness wherein we become cognizant of our own thoughts, emotions, and motivations, serves as a beacon of enlightenment. It is the compass that enables us to navigate the treacherous terrain of our inner selves, granting us a deeper understanding of our emotional landscape. Through self-awareness, we gain clarity, honing our ability to recognize and interpret our emotions, thus becoming better equipped to confront the challenges that arise.

In the face of emotional trials, self-awareness acts as a lighthouse, illuminating the hidden recesses of our minds and allowing us to discern the underlying causes and triggers of our emotional responses. By observing our thoughts and feelings with unwavering honesty, we unlock the door to self-discovery. We gain insights into the intricate interplay between our internal experiences and external stimuli, unraveling the tangled web of emotions that often entangle our decision-making process.

Self-reflection, the companion of self-awareness, propels us further on our journey of emotional navigation. It is the mechanism by which we delve into the depths of our being, seeking wisdom and understanding. Through self-reflection, we engage in a dialogue with ourselves, a profound conversation that unveils the layers of our emotional complexities.

In the midst of emotional challenges, self-reflection offers solace and clarity. It allows us to pause, to step back from the chaos of our emotions, and to examine them with a discerning eye. In these moments of introspection, we confront our own biases, assumptions, and fears, peeling back the layers of our emotional armor. We confront the uncomfortable truths that lie within, acknowledging our vulnerabilities and limitations.

Moreover, self-reflection enables us to cultivate empathy and compassion for ourselves. It grants us the opportunity to nurture a kind and gentle inner dialogue, one that encourages growth and self-acceptance. Through this process, we develop a greater understanding of our emotional patterns, allowing us to respond to challenges with grace and resilience.

Navigating Emotional Challenges: The Power of Self-Awareness and Self-Reflection

The importance of self-awareness and self-reflection in navigating emotional challenges cannot be overstated. They serve as powerful tools in our arsenal, empowering us to make informed decisions and navigate the turbulent seas of our emotions.

When confronted with intense emotions, self-awareness allows us to recognize the physical and psychological manifestations of our emotional states. It provides us with a moment of pause, a space for introspection, in which we can evaluate the impact of our emotions on our thoughts and actions. This heightened self-awareness enables us to disentangle ourselves from the grip of overwhelming emotions, ensuring that our decision-making remains grounded and rational.

Simultaneously, self-reflection serves as a compass in times of emotional turmoil. It prompts us to question our automatic responses, to challenge our preconceived notions, and to explore alternative perspectives. Through this process, we gain a deeper understanding of our emotional triggers and biases. We become attuned to the subtle nuances of our emotional landscape, allowing us to respond with intention rather than react impulsively.

Furthermore, self-reflection fosters personal growth and resilience. It provides us with the opportunity to learn from our experiences, to extract wisdom from our emotional trials. By engaging in honest and introspective dialogue, we can identify patterns, strengths, and areas for improvement. This self-knowledge empowers us to make wiser decisions, to navigate future challenges with greater equanimity.

The significance of self-awareness and self-reflection in navigating emotional challenges is profound. They serve as beacons of light amidst the darkness, guiding us through the treacherous storms of our emotions. Through self-awareness, we gain clarity and understanding, enabling us to recognize and interpret our emotional landscape. Self-reflection, on the other hand, propels us on a journey of self-discovery, granting us the wisdom and resilience to confront emotional trials with grace.

Emotional mastery, the pinnacle of self-control, empowers us to confront the storms of our emotions with grace and resilience. Coping mechanisms serve as allies on this journey, providing us with the tools to manage and regulate our emotional states effectively.

One such mechanism is deep breathing exercises, an artful practice that merges the physical and emotional realms. Through deliberate and conscious breaths, we can anchor ourselves in the present moment, fostering a sense of calm and tranquility. Deep breathing activates the parasympathetic nervous system, counteracting the fight-or-flight response and promoting a state of relaxation. In this state, we gain clarity and perspective, enabling us to approach decision-making with a balanced and composed mind.

Another powerful coping mechanism is journaling, a literary voyage into the depths of our emotions. By putting pen to paper, we embark on a cathartic process of self-expression and introspection. Journaling allows us to externalize our thoughts and feelings, providing a safe space for reflection and release. Through this practice, we gain insights into our emotional patterns, identifying triggers and discovering strategies for emotional regulation. Journaling also serves as a testament to our growth, capturing our journey and serving as a reminder of our resilience.

The importance of coping mechanisms in navigating emotional challenges cannot be overstated. They serve as beacons of light amidst the darkness, guiding us through the tempestuous seas of our emotions. By adopting coping mechanisms, we equip ourselves with the ability to manage and regulate our emotional states effectively.

Deep breathing exercises, for instance, serve as a life raft in times of emotional turmoil. By engaging in intentional and rhythmic breaths, we anchor ourselves in the present, transcending the chaos of our emotions. This practice allows us to distance ourselves from the overwhelming tide of feelings, providing a moment of respite and clarity. Deep breathing cultivates a sense of mindfulness, enabling us to make decisions with a focused and centered mind.

Similarly, journaling serves as a compass, navigating us through the labyrinthine maze of our emotions. Through the act of writing, we externalize our inner landscape, capturing the nuances and intricacies of our emotional experiences. Journaling offers a space for reflection, enabling us to dissect our emotions and uncover their deeper meanings. By engaging in this practice, we develop self-awareness and self-reflection, gaining a deeper understanding of ourselves and our emotional triggers. Journaling also provides an opportunity for catharsis, allowing us to release pent-up emotions and find solace in the written word.

The art of emotional mastery necessitates the employment of coping mechanisms to effectively manage and regulate our emotions. Deep breathing exercises and journaling stand as powerful tools in this endeavor, offering solace, clarity, and introspection. Through the deliberate practice of deep breathing, we ground ourselves in the present moment, fostering a sense of tranquility and balance. Journaling, on the other hand, serves as a literary voyage into the depths of our emotions, facilitating self-expression, self-reflection, and personal growth.

As we navigate the intricacies of decision-making, may we embrace the transformative power of coping mechanisms. By engaging in deep breathing exercises and journaling, we embark on a journey of emotional self-mastery, empowering ourselves to confront the challenges that arise with resilience and grace. Let us honor the wisdom of the ages, adopting these practices as timeless companions on our expedition towards emotional well-being and effective decision-making.

Beyond deep breathing exercises and journaling, there are various other coping mechanisms that can be effective in managing emotions. Here are a few additional strategies:

Mindfulness and Meditation: Mindfulness involves being fully present and aware of the current moment without judgment. Meditation practices, such as mindfulness meditation, can help cultivate a calm and focused state of mind. By observing and accepting our emotions without attachment, we can develop a greater sense of self-awareness and emotional regulation.

Physical Exercise: Engaging in regular physical exercise, whether it's aerobic activities, strength training, or yoga, can have a profound impact on managing emotions. Exercise releases endorphins, which are natural mood boosters, and reduces stress hormones. It provides a healthy outlet for pent-up emotions and promotes overall well-being.

Seeking Support: Sharing our emotions and seeking support from trusted friends, family members, or mental health professionals can provide immense relief. Talking about our feelings allows us to gain perspective, receive validation, and explore potential solutions. Supportive relationships can offer comfort, guidance, and a sense of belonging.

Engaging in Creative Outlets: Artistic expression, such as painting, writing, playing an instrument, or engaging in any creative activity, can serve as a powerful outlet for emotions. Creativity offers a means of self-expression, allowing emotions to be channeled into a tangible form. It can foster self-discovery, healing, and personal growth.

Practicing Self-Care: Taking care of oneself is essential for emotional well-being. Engaging in activities that bring joy and relaxation, such as taking a bath, reading a book, spending time in nature, or engaging in hobbies, can help reduce stress and promote emotional balance. Prioritizing self-care nurtures a positive relationship with oneself and cultivates resilience.

Cognitive Restructuring: Cognitive restructuring involves challenging and reframing negative or distorted thoughts that contribute to emotional distress. By questioning the validity of our thoughts, examining evidence, and replacing negative thoughts with more realistic and positive ones, we can manage our emotions more effectively.

Time Management and Stress Reduction: Effective time management and stress reduction techniques, such as prioritizing tasks, setting boundaries, practicing time-blocking, and engaging in relaxation techniques like progressive muscle relaxation or guided imagery, can alleviate stress and prevent emotional overwhelm.

It's important to note that different coping mechanisms work for different individuals, and it may require some experimentation to find what works best for you. Combining multiple strategies and tailoring them to your unique needs can enhance their effectiveness in managing emotions. Additionally, seeking professional guidance from a therapist or counselor can provide personalized coping strategies and support in navigating emotional challenges.

Confirmation Bias and Expanding Perspectives

Confirmation bias, the subtle manipulator of our thoughts, has a potent impact on decision-making. It is the tendency to seek, interpret, and favor information that confirms pre-existing beliefs or hypotheses. Like a skilled statesman, confirmation bias subtly steers our perceptions, shaping the narrative to align with our preconceived notions.

Confirmation bias plays a pivotal role in decision-making, subtly influencing our judgments and choices. By selectively seeking information that confirms our existing beliefs, we create an echo chamber of ideas, shielding ourselves from alternative viewpoints. This bias hampers our ability to make well-rounded, objective decisions, as it narrows our focus and blinds us to the full spectrum of possibilities.

Confirmation bias is deeply ingrained in the tapestry of human nature, reflecting our innate desire for coherence and consistency. The human mind seeks harmony between its beliefs and the external world, eagerly embracing evidence that supports its preconceptions. This inclination, while rooted in our evolutionary heritage, can lead to a distortion of reality and hinder our capacity for critical thinking.

Confirmation bias operates through various mechanisms, subtly clouding our judgment and reinforcing our existing beliefs. One such mechanism is selective exposure, where we gravitate towards information sources that align with our views, inadvertently shielding ourselves from dissenting opinions. Additionally, we engage in selective perception, interpreting ambiguous information in a manner that confirms our preconceived notions, while dismissing or distorting contradictory evidence.

The influence of confirmation bias on decision-making can have far-reaching consequences. It can lead to premature conclusions, as we accept information that validates our initial hypotheses without sufficient scrutiny. This hampers our ability to consider alternative perspectives and blinds us to the potential risks and opportunities inherent in a decision. Confirmation bias can also fuel groupthink, as like-minded individuals reinforce each other's biases, amplifying the collective blind spots and stifling dissenting voices.

While confirmation bias may be deeply ingrained within us, there are strategies we can employ to mitigate its influence and broaden our perspectives. By actively adopting an open-minded stance and fostering intellectual humility, we can create space for alternative viewpoints and challenge our own assumptions. Actively seeking out diverse opinions, engaging in critical thinking, and encouraging constructive debate can help counter the sway of confirmation bias.

In organizations and communities, fostering a culture of intellectual curiosity and intellectual diversity can serve as a powerful antidote to confirmation bias. Encouraging individuals to question their own biases, inviting dissenting perspectives, and promoting a healthy exchange of ideas can expand our collective understanding and enhance decision-making processes.

Confirmation bias stands as a formidable force, subtly shaping our decision-making processes. It is a product of human nature, rooted in our innate desire for coherence and consistency. Acknowledging its influence is the first step toward overcoming its sway. By actively seeking out diverse perspectives, embracing critical thinking, and fostering intellectual humility, we can transcend the limitations imposed by confirmation bias. Let us honor the wisdom of the ages, adopting these strategies as timeless companions on our expedition toward balanced judgment and effective decision-making.

To embark upon the journey of seeking diverse perspectives, one must first embrace intellectual exploration. Like an intrepid adventurer, we must venture beyond the confines of our own echo chambers and comfort zones, seeking new horizons. This requires a willingness to challenge our own beliefs, to question the status quo, and to immerse ourselves in the vast ocean of knowledge that exists beyond our immediate purview.

In the pursuit of diverse perspectives, intellectual humility becomes a guiding principle. It is the recognition that our own knowledge and understanding are inherently limited, and that others possess valuable insights that can enrich our own understanding. By embracing intellectual humility, we open ourselves up to the wisdom and experiences of others, recognizing that true growth lies in acknowledging the vastness of the intellectual landscape.

Actively seeking diverse voices entails proactively seeking out perspectives that differ from our own. This involves diversifying our sources of information, engaging with individuals from various backgrounds and cultures, and actively listening to their experiences and viewpoints. By expanding the range of voices we encounter, we broaden our understanding of the world and enhance our capacity for empathy and compassion.

Engaging in open and constructive dialogue is a cornerstone of embracing diverse perspectives. Dialogue requires not only the ability to express oneself effectively but also the willingness to listen attentively and respectfully to others. It is through dialogue that ideas are refined, misconceptions are dispelled, and common ground is discovered. By fostering an environment of open dialogue, we create a space where diverse perspectives can flourish and collective wisdom can emerge.

Critical thinking serves as a catalyst for actively seeking diverse perspectives. It is the ability to analyze information objectively, question assumptions, and evaluate evidence. By honing our critical thinking skills, we develop the capacity to discern between valid arguments and fallacious reasoning. This empowers us to engage in meaningful discussions, challenge prevailing narratives, and seek out alternative viewpoints that may have been overlooked.

Intellectual diversity is the lifeblood of vibrant discourse and the key to expanding perspectives. It encompasses a wide range of viewpoints, ideologies, and approaches to problem-solving. By actively nurturing intellectual diversity, we create an environment where contrasting ideas can coexist harmoniously, fostering an atmosphere of innovation, creativity, and mutual respect.

Empathy and perspective-taking are essential tools for actively seeking diverse perspectives. Empathy enables us to understand and share the feelings of others, while perspective-taking allows us to step into someone else's shoes and view the world through their eyes. By cultivating these qualities, we develop a deeper appreciation for the richness and complexity of human experiences, fostering connections and fostering a sense of unity amidst diversity.

Actively seeking diverse perspectives requires embracing discomfort and uncertainty. It necessitates challenging our own biases and confronting ideas that may challenge our preconceived notions. By stepping out of our comfort zones and embracing the unknown, we create opportunities for personal growth and intellectual expansion.

Actively seeking diverse perspectives and engaging in open dialogue is an art that requires courage, intellectual humility, and a genuine commitment to growth. By employing strategies such as embracing intellectual exploration, fostering constructive dialogue, and nurturing intellectual diversity, we pave the way for a more inclusive and enlightened society. Let us embrace the spirit of intellectual curiosity and forge a path toward a future where diverse voices harmoniously coexist, enriching our collective understanding of the world we inhabit.

At the core of intellectual evolution lies the imperative to reassess assumptions and beliefs. It is a process akin to the statesman who ponders the complexities of governance, constantly reevaluating his strategies and policies. By regularly subjecting our assumptions and beliefs to rigorous scrutiny, we pave the way for personal growth, intellectual maturity, and a deeper understanding of the world around us.

Confirmation bias, the subtle architect of our cognitive framework, can hinder our ability to reassess assumptions and beliefs objectively. It is the tendency to favor information that aligns with our preexisting convictions, shielding us from alternative perspectives. To overcome this innate inclination, we must summon the courage to challenge our own biases, peering through the lens of intellectual honesty to uncover new vistas of knowledge.

Assumptions and beliefs are not immutable entities, but rather fluid constructs subject to the ebb and flow of intellectual tides. The pursuit of truth demands that we acknowledge the transient nature of our convictions. Like the ever-changing landscape that inspired the great artists of yore, truth reveals itself through an ongoing dialogue between inquiry and revision.

To embark upon the path of reassessing assumptions and beliefs, one must embrace the virtues of humility and intellectual curiosity. Humility enables us to recognize the limitations of our understanding, fostering an openness to new ideas and perspectives. Intellectual curiosity, akin to the relentless explorer, propels us forward, urging us to venture beyond the boundaries of our current knowledge.

Reassessing assumptions and beliefs necessitates a mindset of continuous learning. It is a journey that demands the tireless pursuit of knowledge, the unyielding spirit of the inquisitive scholar. By cultivating a thirst for learning, we expand the boundaries of our intellectual landscape, welcoming the winds of change and embracing the transformative power of new insights.

Critical thinking assumes a central role in the process of reassessing assumptions and beliefs. It is the art of analyzing information objectively, questioning assumptions, and evaluating evidence with discerning eyes. By honing our critical thinking skills, we develop the capacity to challenge deeply ingrained notions, dismantling intellectual barriers and paving the way for profound intellectual growth.

Reassessing assumptions and beliefs demands that we confront the discomfort of uncertainty. It requires us to venture into the uncharted territories of the unknown, shedding the cloak of complacency that stifles intellectual progress. Like the intrepid voyager navigating treacherous seas, we must embrace the uncertainty that accompanies the pursuit of truth, trusting in our capacity to adapt and grow amidst the shifting currents of knowledge.

Regularly reassessing assumptions and beliefs liberates us from the confines of intellectual stagnation. It awakens us to the vastness of human knowledge, igniting a fire within that propels us toward intellectual emancipation. By freeing ourselves from the shackles of dogma, we create space for intellectual exploration, embracing the transformative potential that lies in the continuous reassessment of our assumptions and beliefs.

Regularly reassessing assumptions and beliefs empowers us to challenge the status quo. It is through questioning the established norms and conventional wisdom that progress is made. Like the visionary reformer, we have the opportunity to transcend the boundaries of societal constraints and pave the way for innovation and positive change. By critically examining our assumptions, we open ourselves up to the possibility of disrupting outdated paradigms and forging new paths.

Reassessing assumptions and beliefs cultivates intellectual resilience within us. In a rapidly evolving world where knowledge is ever-expanding, it is crucial to adapt and evolve our perspectives accordingly. By embracing a mindset of continual reassessment, we develop the ability to weather the storms of intellectual challenges, adapt to new information, and refine our understanding. This resilience allows us to navigate the complexities of an ever-changing landscape with intellectual acuity and flexibility.

Regularly reassessing assumptions and beliefs serves as a testament to our intellectual integrity. It demonstrates our commitment to truth-seeking and intellectual honesty. By examining our beliefs with a critical eye, we demonstrate a willingness to confront potential inconsistencies or biases. This process requires us to set aside ego and embrace the pursuit of knowledge above personal attachment to any particular belief. Through intellectual integrity, we foster an environment of intellectual rigor and cultivate a reputation for sound judgment and intellectual credibility.

Reassessing assumptions and beliefs fosters empathy and understanding towards others. It allows us to step into different perspectives, to see the world through diverse lenses. By challenging our own assumptions, we develop a deeper appreciation for the nuances and complexities of the human experience. This enhanced empathy enables us to engage in more meaningful and compassionate interactions, bridging divides and fostering a sense of unity amidst diversity.

Regular reassessment of assumptions and beliefs unleashes the power of creativity and innovation within us. By breaking free from the constraints of rigid thinking, we open ourselves up to new ideas and possibilities. Just as the artist experiments with different colors and techniques, we explore uncharted intellectual territories. This exploration fuels our imagination, enabling us to think outside the box, challenge conventional boundaries, and create novel solutions to complex problems.

The process of reassessing assumptions and beliefs is an avenue for personal growth and self-discovery. As we engage in self-reflection, we gain deeper insights into our own values, biases, and aspirations. This introspection allows us to refine our sense of self and align our beliefs with our evolving understanding of the world. Through this journey of self-discovery, we unlock hidden potentials, embrace personal growth, and embark on a transformative path towards becoming our best selves.

Regular reassessment of assumptions and beliefs empowers us intellectually. It liberates us from the constraints of dogma and encourages us to think independently. By taking ownership of our beliefs and subjecting them to critical scrutiny, we become active participants in the pursuit of knowledge. This sense of intellectual empowerment instills within us a confidence to engage in informed discussions, contribute to meaningful debates, and advocate for ideas that are grounded in reason and evidence.

The importance of regularly reassessing assumptions and beliefs extends beyond intellectual growth. It challenges the status quo, fosters resilience and integrity, enhances empathy and understanding, unleashes creativity and innovation, nurtures personal growth, and cultivates intellectual empowerment. By embarking on this journey of self-reflection, we unlock the potential for profound transformation and contribute to the collective pursuit of truth and enlightenment.

Multitasking and Cultivating Single-Tasking Skills

In a world brimming with distractions and incessant demands for our attention, the art of single-tasking emerges as a resolute antidote to the perils of multitasking.

In a society fixated on productivity and efficiency, multitasking has been exalted as a symbol of accomplishment. However, beneath its guise lies the fallacy of divided attention. Multitasking, the frenetic endeavor of juggling multiple tasks simultaneously, dilutes our focus, fractures our concentration, and compromises the quality of our work. To escape this quagmire, we must embrace the art of single-tasking, a practice that channels our energy into a singular endeavor, fostering deeper engagement, heightened efficiency, and superior outcomes.

Contrary to popular belief, multitasking does not bestow superhuman productivity. Instead, it leads to a diminished capacity to perform tasks effectively. By attempting to tackle multiple tasks at once, we become mired in a state of perpetual busyness, yet our progress remains stagnant. Single-tasking, on the other hand, allows us to direct our undivided attention towards a solitary task, unlocking the potential for heightened focus, increased productivity, and a greater sense of accomplishment.

Single-tasking harnesses the power of focused attention, akin to the statesman who dedicates his unwavering focus to the weightiest matters of governance. When we immerse ourselves fully in a single task, we enter a state of flow, where time seems to dissolve, and our efforts become seamless and effortless. This state of deep concentration enables us to achieve optimal performance, unlocking our untapped potential and fostering a sense of fulfillment in our endeavors.

In a digital age teeming with distractions, cultivating single-tasking skills becomes an act of defiance against the siren call of constant stimulation. The allure of social media notifications, email pings, and the incessant buzz of modern life can hijack our attention, fragmenting our focus into scattered fragments. By consciously choosing to resist these distractions and redirect our attention towards a singular task, we regain control over our cognitive resources and create a space for deep work and profound insights.

Single-tasking cultivates cognitive agility, the capacity to seamlessly transition between different mental states and tasks. By honing our ability to allocate our attention effectively, we become adept at focusing on the task at hand, filtering out irrelevant stimuli, and swiftly shifting gears as necessary. This agility enables us to adapt to changing demands, seize opportunities for innovation, and demonstrate mental dexterity akin to the consummate statesman navigating the complexities of diplomacy.

Single-tasking is an avenue for embracing mindfulness and presence in our daily lives. By immersing ourselves fully in the present moment, we tap into the richness of our experiences, savoring each task with undivided attention. This practice instills a sense of calm amidst the chaos, allowing us to connect deeply with our work, our surroundings, and the people around us. Through mindfulness, we foster a profound appreciation for the beauty and intricacies of each moment, infusing our endeavors with a sense of purpose and meaning.

Cultivating single-tasking skills requires deliberate effort and the establishment of supportive habits. By setting clear priorities, breaking tasks into manageable chunks, and eliminating distractions, we create an environment conducive to focused attention. Additionally, incorporating rituals and routines into our workflow can signal our brains to enter a state of concentration, facilitating the seamless transition into single-tasking mode. With practice and discipline, single-tasking becomes a natural and empowering way of approaching our work and daily activities.

While single-tasking is essential for individual productivity, it is crucial to strike a balance between solitary focus and collaborative endeavors. Just as the statesman consults advisors and engages in diplomatic negotiations, we must recognize the value of collaboration and collective problem-solving. By leveraging the strengths and perspectives of others, we enrich our own understanding and elevate the quality of our work. The art lies in knowing when to immerse ourselves in solitary focus and when to embrace collaboration for optimal outcomes.

Multitasking, the art of juggling multiple tasks simultaneously, has become a revered symbol of accomplishment. Like a statesman orchestrating the intricacies of governance, we attempt to manage an array of responsibilities in a fragmented manner. However, the allure of multitasking masks the truth beneath its surface. It creates an illusion of effectiveness while compromising the quality of our work, fracturing our attention, and impeding our ability to fully engage with each task at hand.

Multitasking exacts a significant toll on our cognitive faculties. Rather than enhancing efficiency, it fragments our attention into scattered fragments, leading to suboptimal performance. The statesman, immersed in the weightiest matters of governance, understands the importance of undivided focus. Similarly, single-tasking allows us to direct our attention towards a singular endeavor, enabling us to reach a state of flow and optimal performance. Multitasking, on the other hand, spreads our cognitive resources thin, resulting in diminished productivity and compromised decision-making.

Contrary to popular belief, multitasking does not bestow superiority in performance. It creates an illusion of accomplishment, fostering a false sense of productivity. The statesman, with his unwavering focus on the most pressing issues, achieves remarkable feats through single-minded dedication. In our pursuit of multitasking, we deceive ourselves into believing that we are achieving more when, in reality, we are merely scratching the surface of our true potential.

Multitasking undermines our ability to make sound decisions. The statesman, renowned for his discerning judgment, recognizes the importance of focused attention when faced with complex choices. Multitasking, with its fragmented focus and divided resources, impairs our capacity to consider options critically, analyze information thoroughly, and weigh the consequences of our decisions. It renders us susceptible to errors, oversights, and hasty judgments, jeopardizing the quality and efficacy of our choices.

The pursuit of multitasking in the name of productivity becomes a paradoxical endeavor. While we strive to accomplish more in less time, the fragmented nature of multitasking hampers our ability to complete tasks efficiently and effectively. The statesman, with his strategic approach to governance, understands the importance of prioritization and focused effort. Similarly, by embracing single-tasking, we channel our energy into one task at a time, unlocking the potential for heightened productivity, improved quality, and a sense of fulfillment in our achievements.

Multitasking requires constant switching of attention between tasks, a cognitive endeavor that comes at a cost. The statesman, with his judicious allocation of resources, recognizes the value of continuity in thought and action. Multitasking, however, disrupts this continuity, as we shift gears abruptly and attempt to reorient ourselves repeatedly.

Each instance of switching incurs a cognitive overhead, depleting our mental reserves and impeding our ability to perform at our best.

To reclaim our productivity and enhance our decision-making prowess, we must embrace the art of single-tasking. Like the statesman engrossed in the weightiest matters of governance, we focus our attention on one task at a time, immersing ourselves fully in its intricacies. Single-tasking allows us to enter a state of flow, where time becomes elastic, distractions fade away, and our efforts become seamless and purposeful. It empowers us to allocate our cognitive resources effectively, enabling us to accomplish tasks with heightened efficiency and precision.

Cultivating single-tasking skills requires deliberate effort and the establishment of supportive habits. We must resist the allure of constant distraction and create an environment conducive to focused attention. The statesman, with his disciplined approach to governance, provides inspiration for the cultivation of such habits. By setting clear priorities, eliminating distractions, and embracing mindfulness, we create the conditions necessary for single-tasking to flourish. Through practice and discipline, we can gradually rewire our cognitive patterns and unlock the transformative potential of single-taskingin our lives.

Mindfulness serves as a guiding principle in our journey towards embracing single-tasking. As we detach ourselves from the noise of constant stimulation, we cultivate a heightened sense of awareness and presence. The statesman, with his acute perception of the political landscape, exemplifies the power of mindfulness in decision-making. By immersing ourselves fully in the present moment, we connect deeply with each task, harnessing our focus, and imbuing our actions with intention and purpose.

In an era defined by technological advancements, we must navigate the digital landscape with discernment. The statesman, with his diplomatic prowess, understands the importance of utilizing tools judiciously. Similarly, we must embrace technology as an aid rather than a hindrance to single-tasking. By leveraging productivity tools, time management apps, and digital boundaries, we create a harmonious relationship between technology and our pursuit of focused attention.

While single-tasking empowers individual productivity, collaboration remains a cornerstone of human progress. The statesman, with his adeptness in negotiation and coalition-building, exemplifies the power of collaboration. Single-tasking does not advocate for isolation but rather encourages a balanced approach. We must discern when to engage in collaborative endeavors, leveraging the diverse perspectives and expertise of others to enrich our own understanding. By striking a harmonious balance between solitary focus and collaborative efforts, we optimize our potential for achievement and decision-making.

Cultivating single-tasking skills is a journey towards mastery. The statesman, with his lifelong pursuit of diplomacy, serves as a testament to the rewards of dedicated practice. Similarly, by committing ourselves to the art of single-tasking, we embark on a transformative path. It requires patience, discipline, and a willingness to confront the allure of multitasking. Through consistent effort and an unwavering commitment to focused attention, we gradually master the art of single-tasking, unlocking our true potential and reaping the benefits in all areas of our lives.

In the contemporary milieu, where the demands of life are as diverse as they are numerous, the ability to multitask is often lauded as a virtue.

The concept of multitasking, or the simultaneous execution of multiple tasks, is a fallacy. In reality, the human brain engages in task-switching, rapidly shifting focus from one task to another. This constant shifting can lead to cognitive overload, diminished productivity, and increased stress levels.

In contrast, single-tasking, the practice of focusing on one task at a time, can enhance productivity, reduce stress, and improve the quality of work. It is a skill that can be cultivated and refined, much like a master craftsman hones his art.

One technique that has gained significant traction in promoting single-tasking is the Pomodoro Technique. Named after the tomato-shaped kitchen timer used by its creator, Francesco Cirillo, this method is a testament to the power of simplicity.

The Pomodoro Technique involves breaking work into intervals, traditionally 25 minutes in length, separated by short breaks. Each interval is known as a 'Pomodoro'. After four Pomodoros, a longer break is taken. This method encourages focused work during the Pomodoros and provides regular intervals for mental rejuvenation.

The beauty of the Pomodoro Technique lies in its simplicity and adaptability. It can be applied to any task, from writing a report to studying for an exam. The technique also fosters a sense of accomplishment, as each completed Pomodoro represents a tangible achievement.

Another technique that promotes single-tasking is the 'Two-Minute Rule'. Popularized by productivity expert David Allen, this rule states that if a task can be completed in two minutes or less, it should be done immediately. This rule prevents the accumulation of small tasks that can clutter the mind and distract from larger tasks.

The 'Two-Minute Rule' is a powerful tool for cultivating a single-tasking mindset. It encourages immediate action, reducing the temptation to multitask and promoting a focus on the task at hand.

In addition to these techniques, creating a conducive environment is crucial for single-tasking. This includes eliminating distractions, such as turning off notifications on electronic devices, and creating a physical space that promotes focus.

The cultivation of mindfulness can also enhance single-tasking skills. Mindfulness, the practice of being fully present and engaged in the current task, can improve focus and reduce the temptation to multitask. It can be cultivated through practices such as meditation and yoga, or simply by making a conscious effort to focus on the present moment.

While multitasking may seem like an efficient use of time, it often leads to decreased productivity and increased stress. The cultivation of single-tasking skills, through techniques such as the Pomodoro Technique and the 'Two-Minute Rule', can enhance productivity, reduce stress, and improve the quality of work.

The art of single-tasking is not a skill that can be mastered overnight. It requires patience, practice, and a commitment to focusing on one task at a time. However, with time and persistence, the rewards are significant. As the famous saying goes, "Rome was not built in a day." Similarly, the skill of single-tasking is built over time, one focused task at a time.

One of the key advantages of single-tasking is the ability to give our full attention to a particular task. When we attempt to juggle multiple tasks at once, our focus is divided, resulting in decreased efficiency and quality of work. By dedicating focused time to each activity, we can immerse ourselves fully in the task at hand and produce higher-quality output.

In addition to improved focus, single-tasking can also lead to increased creativity and innovation. When we allow ourselves the time and space to fully engage with a task, we are more likely to come up with new ideas and solutions. By minimizing distractions and honing our ability to concentrate on one thing at a time, we can unlock our creative potential and think more critically about the problems we are trying to solve.

Furthermore, setting dedicated time for each activity can help us manage our workload more effectively. By breaking our day into focused blocks of time dedicated to specific tasks, we can prioritize our work and ensure that we are making progress on key projects. This can lead to a sense of accomplishment and satisfaction as we see tangible results from our efforts.

In addition to improving our productivity and creativity, single-tasking can also have a positive impact on our mental health. In today's digital age, we are constantly bombarded with distractions and notifications that can take a toll on our well-being. By intentionally carving out time for focused work and minimizing external interruptions, we can create a sense of calm and control in our lives.

While multitasking may seem like the more efficient approach, research suggests that it can actually be detrimental to our overall performance. By embracing single-tasking and dedicating focused time to each activity, we can maximize our productivity, creativity, and mental well-being. In a world that values constant busyness and distraction, cultivating our single-tasking skills can be a powerful antidote to the chaos of modern life.

The choice between multitasking and single-tasking is not a binary one. Both have their place and can be used effectively depending on the situation. However, in a world that often values quantity over quality, it is essential to remember the value of focusing on one task at a time.

Overcoming Mind Challenges for Success

In the pursuit of success, it is common to strive for perfection. However, this relentless quest for flawlessness can often lead to mind challenges that hinder rather than help our progress.

Perfectionism, or the relentless pursuit of flawlessness, is a common mind challenge that many individuals face. While striving for excellence can be a positive motivator, the pressure to be perfect can lead to fear of failure, procrastination, and decreased productivity. It can also lead to a negative self-image and decreased well-being, as individuals constantly compare themselves to unrealistic standards.

In contrast, embracing imperfections can lead to increased creativity, resilience, and well-being. This involves accepting that mistakes are a natural part of the learning process and that no one is perfect. It also involves recognizing that imperfections can often lead to unique and innovative solutions, rather than being a sign of failure.

One key aspect of embracing imperfections is learning from mistakes. Rather than viewing mistakes as failures, individuals can view them as opportunities for growth and learning. This involves analyzing the mistake to understand what went wrong, identifying lessons learned, and developing strategies to prevent similar mistakes in the future.

Another key aspect of embracing imperfections is practicing self-compassion. Self-compassion involves treating oneself with kindness, understanding, and forgiveness, rather than harsh self-criticism. It also involves recognizing that everyone makes mistakes and that imperfections are a part of the human experience.

Practicing self-compassion can lead to increased resilience, well-being, and productivity. It can also lead to improved relationships with others, as individuals who are kind to themselves are often kinder to others as well.

To embrace imperfections and practice self-compassion, individuals can employ various strategies. One such strategy is mindfulness, or the practice of being present and aware in the current moment. Mindfulness can help individuals to accept their imperfections, rather than dwelling on them or trying to ignore them.

Another strategy is positive self-talk, or the practice of speaking to oneself in a kind and supportive manner. Positive self-talk can help to counteract the negative self-talk that often accompanies perfectionism and can lead to increased self-compassion.

Individuals can practice gratitude, or the act of focusing on and appreciating the positive aspects of life. Gratitude can help to shift the focus away from imperfections and towards the positive aspects of oneself and one's life.

Managing mental fatigue can be a challenging task, requiring a strategic approach to ensure success. In our fast-paced and demanding world, it is crucial to prioritize self-care and relaxation strategies in order to combat the effects of mental exhaustion. By establishing a consistent sleep routine and incorporating physical activity into our daily lives, we can effectively manage mental fatigue and boost our overall well-being.

Self-care is a crucial aspect of managing mental fatigue, as it allows us to recharge and rejuvenate our minds and bodies. By prioritizing activities that bring us joy and relaxation, such as meditation, yoga, or spending time in nature, we can reduce stress and improve our mental resilience. Taking time for ourselves and engaging in activities that promote self-care can help us to overcome the challenges of mental fatigue and maintain a healthy balance in our lives.

In addition to self-care, establishing a consistent sleep routine is essential for managing mental fatigue. Quality sleep is crucial for cognitive function and overall well-being, and lack of sleep can significantly impact our mental performance and alertness. By creating a bedtime routine and ensuring that we get an adequate amount of rest each night, we can enhance our ability to focus and concentrate, ultimately reducing the effects of mental fatigue.

Physical activity is another key component in managing mental fatigue, as exercise has been shown to have a positive impact on mood, energy levels, and cognitive function. Incorporating regular physical activity into our daily lives can help to reduce stress, improve our mental clarity, and boost our overall sense of well-being. Whether it's going for a walk, practicing yoga, or engaging in a more intense workout, finding ways to move our bodies can have a profound effect on our mental resilience and ability to overcome challenges.

Overall, managing mental fatigue requires a holistic approach that prioritizes self-care, consistent sleep, and regular physical activity. By implementing these strategies into our daily routines, we can enhance our mental resilience, improve our focus and concentration, and ultimately achieve success in overcoming the challenges of mental fatigue.

Fear of failure is a common obstacle that many people face when pursuing their goals and dreams. It is the intense feeling of apprehension or worry about failing to achieve a desired outcome. This fear can manifest itself in various aspects of life, such as in relationships, career, personal development, and more.

Examples of fear of failure can include not taking risks or trying new things due to the fear of not succeeding, feeling anxious or stressed about making mistakes, or constantly seeking perfection to avoid failure. It can also lead to procrastination, self-doubt, low self-esteem, and ultimately, a lack of fulfillment in life.

The causes of the fear of failure can stem from various sources, such as past experiences of criticism or rejection, pressure from external sources like family or society, unrealistic expectations of perfection, or a fixed mindset that views failure as a reflection of one's abilities. The consequences of this fear can be detrimental, leading to missed opportunities, stagnation in personal growth, and a feeling of being stuck in a cycle of fear and avoidance.

To overcome the fear of failure, it is essential to reframe failure as an opportunity for growth and learning. By shifting one's perspective on failure, it can be seen as a valuable experience that provides lessons and insights for future success. Embracing failure as a natural part of the journey towards success can help alleviate the fear and reduce its hold on one's mindset.

Setting small, attainable goals can also be a helpful strategy for overcoming the fear of failure. Breaking down larger goals into manageable steps can make them less intimidating and more achievable. By celebrating small wins along the way, it can boost confidence and motivation to continue moving forward despite the fear of failure.

Developing a growth mindset is another key strategy for overcoming the fear of failure. A growth mindset recognizes that abilities and intelligence can be developed through effort and perseverance. By embracing challenges, learning from mistakes, and seeking feedback, individuals with a growth mindset can overcome obstacles and achieve their goals more effectively.

Overall, the fear of failure is a common struggle that many people face, but with the right strategies and mindset, it can be overcome. By reframing failure as an opportunity for growth, setting small, attainable goals, and developing a growth mindset, individuals can conquer their fear of failure and pursue their dreams with confidence and resilience.

Overcoming mental obstacles for success requires dedication, perseverance, and a positive mindset. By recognizing and challenging your negative thoughts, setting clear goals, practicing self-care, and seeking support from others, you can overcome any challenges that come your way. Remember, success is not defined by the absence of obstacles but by your ability to overcome them. Stay focused, stay motivated, and keep pushing forward towards your goals. You have the power to overcome any obstacle that stands in your way.

Disclaimer

The information provided in this book is for educational and informational purposes only. The author and publisher have made every effort to ensure that the information in this book is accurate and up-to-date at the time of publishing, but they make no representations or warranties with respect to the accuracy, applicability, fitness, or completeness of the contents of this book.

The advice and strategies contained herein may not be suitable for every situation. The author and publisher disclaim any liability for any loss or damage caused by the use or misuse of the information contained in this book.

This book is not intended to replace professional advice, whether medical, legal, financial, or otherwise. If professional assistance is required, the services of a competent professional person should be sought.

The author and publisher shall not be liable for any special, incidental, consequential, or indirect damages arising directly or indirectly from the use of this book.

About the Author

Maher Asaad Baker (In Arabic: ماهر أسعد بكر), is a Syrian musician, author, journalist, VFX & graphic artist, and director. He was born in Damascus in 1977. He grew up with a dream of being one of the most well-known artists in the world, and he has been working hard to achieve it ever since.

He started his career in 1997 when he was only 20 years old. He had a passion for technology and media, and he taught himself how to develop applications and websites. He also explored various types of media-creating paths, such as music production, graphic design, video editing, animation, and filmmaking. He was not satisfied with just being a consumer of media; he wanted to be a creator of media.

Reading was another source of inspiration for him. He was always surrounded by books as a child, thanks to his father's extensive library. He read books from different genres, topics, and perspectives. He read books for knowledge, for wisdom, for entertainment, for enlightenment. Reading stimulated his imagination and curiosity. Reading also developed his writing skills.

He did not start writing professionally until later in his life, as he was busy with other projects and pursuits. But when he did start writing, he proved himself to be a talented and prolific writer. He wrote articles for various newspapers and magazines on topics such as politics, culture, society, art, technology, and more. He wrote books that were informative and insightful. He wrote books that were creative and captivating. He wrote books that were best-selling and award-winning.

He is most known for his book "How I wrote a million Wikipedia articles", where he shares his experience of being one of the most prolific contributors to the online encyclopedia. He reveals his methods, techniques, strategies, and secrets of writing high-quality articles on any subject in record time. He also discusses the benefits and challenges of being a Wikipedia editor in the age of information overload.

He is also known for his novel "Becoming the man", where he tells the story of a young man who goes through a series of transformations in his life. The novel explores themes such as identity, masculinity, self-discovery, love, loss, and redemption. The novel is based on his journey to becoming who he is today.

Copyright © 2024 Maher Asaad Baker